For JSB and Family

and
for

Loen and Sho

TC Buell

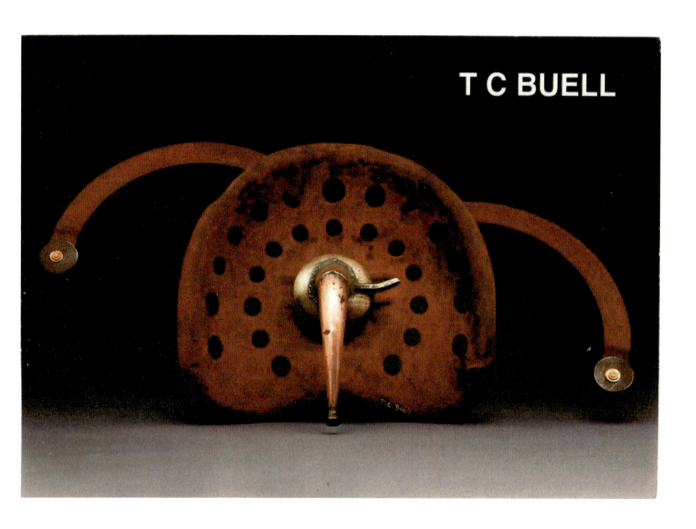

Endangered Species

After Fifteen Years Have Turned

The throaty raven speaks
at first in dreams and when
he comes, speaking in tongues,
he will not translate.

We slide from sleep.
The frieze of sound begins
to render.

Ankle deep in moss and fog,
we do not pick the deadly amanita.
Risk red tide, but avoid its clammy
breath, fear its tingling lips.

Something good will happen
today, she says.

Much stays secret, between us.

Like the balance point
of cormorants, their bent necks
angling like forks.

Each logwood drift turns back
the years we first camped
along this curve of time.

Here's a quiet place to think
why insects make funnel patterns
in the dust.

We know how such questions
are a trap to fall in,
raveling up in words.
And why the seals clap awake
the heron-shrouded night.

More by far is secret.

Like the thrush's privacy.
Swainson's, shy of sharing,
too mute for ears and gone
if scrutinized so closely.

From such notes, if taken well,
the next step might be up
the scale to clearing.

Morning fog moving
off the distant straits.

Totem

America Will Never!

Look out, here she comes again riding

the waves as usual, indifferent to our

lack of caution. And that's the problem.

Heaven forbid we should forget ourselves:

The frogbound pond observes our nakedness.

Perhaps their amber eyes relax us for the

axe and Amy Simple rides to give our Granny

forty smacks. We lie in myriads so sleek.

Come, let us anoint ourselves with oil and

seek the holy whale. But then she lisps,

"Where's the men's women?" Ah, there in the

sky some transcendental pizza, laminate of sun.

And we almost choke on clusters, many marbles.

You count them. I am tired of lying to you.

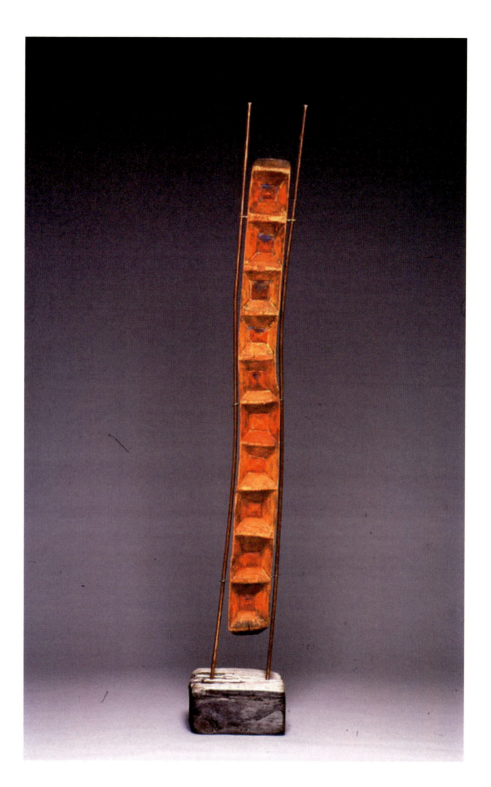

All the Spices of the Orient

Antique Roadshow Bride

Have you any idea how much . . . ?
Not the vaguest, got her 45 years ago.
Can you tell me what you paid for her?
I don't want to say right off.
But here's a hint: There was no dowry.
Yes, well, we usually start with the appraisal.
In any case, in specimens like these we
look carefully to establish authenticity.
Clearly this is not a reproduction.
Note these worm holes. No drilling here.
Only time will do it. And the crowning is real.
Yes, I know that. They threw away the mold
when they made her, and there's no cloning yet.
And note the sagging here. That's real.
And the wrinkling there, the way leather does
even properly treated. We look for that. And look,
no tuckings, no cheating. Absolutely real.
Yes, yes, and that's the beauty of it. I'm just
the same. Look at me. Turkey neck. Elephant behind.
All leathery. All gobbley.
Yes, and again, not your own worm holes.
Impossible to replicate that. Only years will tell.
Like your ears. Have you noted the lengthening
of the lobes? Have you noted that?
I have and I pray to Buddha every day for that.
I call it aging playfully. You know what I mean?
Yes, ah, yes. Impossible to . . . ah, yes, that's the dust
in us, the way of beatles . . . the death watch.
Yes, yes. They remind us of our youth -- no drilling
for any fountain can replicate that, he, heh, can it?
Hee, hee. For you, too. And note your own crowns.
Open wide, now, don't try to hide them. We keep a sharp
eye out for those. Have you any idea what these alone
are worth, not to mention hers?
Do we ever! $650 a drill less insurance times many.
You count 'em, you do the math. How many K? You add up.
OK Ok Ok Let's not go inflationary. It's my turn:
Big question now: She. Not You. She. Have you any idea
what She might be worth. Hung up on the wall? At MOMA?
Indeed I do (aggressively) wise guy. PRICELESS! NFS!
I guess I better believe it. Heh. Heh. 'Nuf said, he said.

Adam and Eve

Any Other Pasture

Yesterday, the heat, today
the rain begins. The moles
busy in their labyrinths
move mountains.

Our dog wears tight lips
in a wise face.

The tumor had blossomed
overnight. Deeper than
nature's claw, there has
been much cutting and sewing.
The plastic bucket over
her head keeps her from chewing
like a trapped coyote.

To restore the corrugated flesh
we try comfrey, even, taken
from the woods. The vet's faith,
foolish as our nostrums,
works no better.

One corner of the wound
sighs as she breathes.
Her nose a compass, she moves
like a bent shopping cart.
The bucket keeps her from seeing.
She blunders and trips on old scents.

We know nothing will work.

This is a secret we would like
to keep from ourselves. Our eyes
look for another language.
The rules for any other pasture
seem more reasonable.

The vet's needle
would be an opening gate.

Turn Out Light at Daybreak

Atlantic Crossing

For NDH

Knuckles nut tight on the wheel,
running my mantra like an outboard.
Like the time I'd fallen in, alone,
in the middle of the pond,
breaking my way to the edge.

I'll make it home, I'll make it sure,
running there with skates still on,
over the frozen fields.

Or the first time I prayed,
my white rat lying senseless
on the bed from when I hit him hard
with a sockfull of BB' s because
he'd half eaten the starling I'd
saved, fallen from its nest.

(The rat, righting itself, blinked pink.)

And you, the skipper, tallest teller
of any tale, you were speechless
in the banshee night, storm trys'l set
running before a full gale, and I
needing blather to keep my mind
from broaching, pitchpoling, giving in.

My mantra half in gear now and slipping,
over the edge, and you, the skipper
catatonic. But no,
you gray-beard loon, you were asleep.
half awash but sleeping. If you
could have that much faith,
then I could too, and tell the tale.

The Munch Twins

The Bases Always Loaded

At Fenway that salt fogged summer
The small boy watches the pitcher poised
to throw
[stopaction]
The ball always in midair, no one ever scoring
the Redsox way behind as usual, the same derisive
tune, organistic--
when suddenly a huge insect appears glued
to the backstop, huge beyond belief--spinning:
But it is only the small boy's schoolmarm
knitting up time again, her sow's lips pursed
for punishment, for his cutting up:
"'tis tiresome, child, 'tis tiresome!"
The boy (bored) overindulges in hotdogs and barfs
them up under the arches along the Charles,
river of discontent
[start action slow motion]
The long summer gone at last, older now
in the back seat of the Chevy with running boards
his hat blows away on Storrow Drive--
[world serious]
No more spitballs. No more teacher's dirty looks.
Hardball now and Pirates. No longer in the minors.
Gone to his majority. Bases loaded up.
[fast forward]
Long since a man, he remains a fan for life
and he hears the deep diapason of his hips
sprocket wrenched by time and he can only see
his toes when he has his trousers rolled.
[playback]
Fenway again. Same old spiders.

American Tourist

Buzzard's Bay at Breakfast

US Weather Bureau displays storm warnings
Hen and Chickens Sow and Pigs
Swept clear to depth indicated
Soundings in fathoms heights in feet
Above mean low water Tuckernut
Menemsha Bight position doubtful Penikese
Existence doubtful minutes seconds
Gravel grass sand shells
Wrecks may be dangerous to surface navigation
Non dangerous wrecks have been omitted
Unexploded depth charge breakers maelstrom

Caution: This chart not intended for navigation

American Tourist Also

Colt Flight 45

I was never any good at math,
but from 40,000 feet the land's
geometry seems plain enough
and the mountains just as solid
and bicentennial. East to West
or West to East, even at 600 mph
the Mason-Dixon line stays put
and the Great Divide stops north
of the border where it should,
depending on weather or not,
and that's a big off-course.

Most days it's clear enough criss-
crossing (call it skull-and-boning)
the sky to see why the Rockies lie
the way they do, or why the mountain
men scalped the rivers clean of beaver
for all their pelts' worth, or why
we have no passenger pigeons, only 747's.

Yes, at 40,000 it's clear enough
how we've dry-gulched the land and
ripsawed the air so long we've
forgotten why we call our cars
horses and our football teams
Cowboys and Indians, or Jets.

Forty degrees below outside's
no joke, could trigger new optometry.

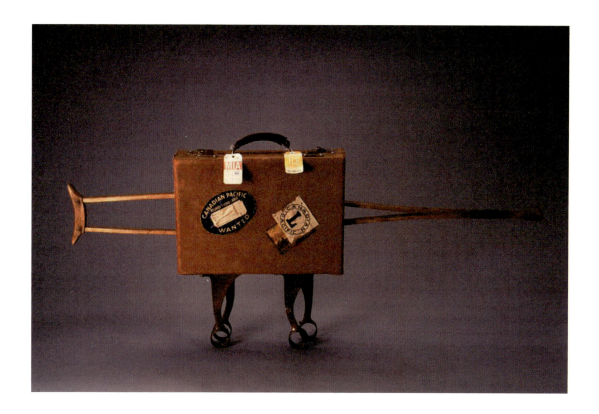

Crutched Tourist

The Crossing

Crossing east by Ford
the days are just as long
as sailing west by wagon
except it takes us six
instead of sixty days.
Exhausted more by trucks
than dust. We lose no children.
An easy time we have of it,
hardly worth the telling.

The first time across
was something else in Kansas,
I mean, the night Judy Garland died.
We met twisters near Salina
and rode them out, dogs and all,
thinking of Dorothy and Oz.
Dragged anchor in our van,
lassoed a Winnebago and ran aground
kneedeep in jackrabbits and hailstones
as big as prairie chickens.

A double rainbow arched the freeway,
and there we saw a fleet of full
rigged trucks disappear forever
through the transcendental scud
of fliptop cans and blown-out tires.

We had to be there to believe it--
the fathoms of corn, the swell of wheat,
the endless roll and fiery ribbons
of the night.

The first crossing tells the best
and lasts longest. On crossings after
that, there's no returning to the past,
except as we imagine it.

19

Ibid

E PLURIBUS UNIVAC

Oh, new found land,
forgive our debtor cards
and deliver us from greenstamps,
that our indentured souls
may find the safest way
to pay and save us
from ourselves.

Ah, men. Oh, women.

Lame Duck Press

Everything's Devouring Almost Everything

I saw Sir David re-run last night,
enballooned, risking vultures.
On Public Television—BBC—PBS
Above our living/dying planet --
"Here we are," he shrills, hovering --
"Here we are, held up by nothing!"

Lions by the pride feast at will on Wildebeasts
and then the camera pans to spearfish leaping clear
of sharks in frenzy, and turtles newly hatched
Skua-scraped from Galapagos beaches --
prime time scream in living color, reds and blues
of tooth and claw, from Serengeti to the Pole.

Everything's devouring almost everything,
regurgitations for each others' nestlings.

Sir David, let us pray, will not be eaten
(so far, he's exceeded Nature's Laws.)

Nor may he never feast upon his brother
the only other Battenborough.

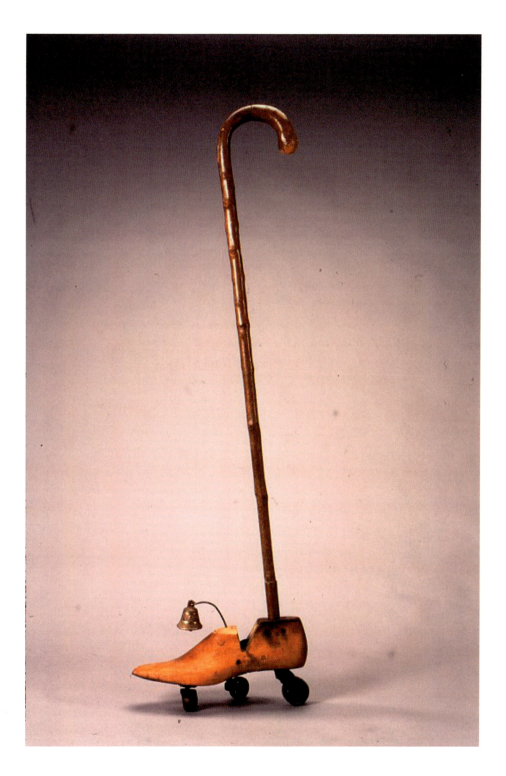

Walking Stick with Warning Bell

For My Wife, My Life

The best thing about being married for fifty years
Is that being married for that long may well be for good.

Then years later in the heavens of our intentions
We might find ourselves still here, amongst ourselves
And others in words and deeds, lovingly.

Let us hope what we have said and done will not
Be held against us. Let me tell this to you now,
Not on tiptoes of the night but in broad
Daylight, rejoicing in the day, best Joan of all—
Lush heart, ripe as lips, fifty years together
And still voyaging, fewer misprints, easier going.

Let's meet at the trailhead and wait to see.

Your Tom

Feather Vane

Global Village: Tribal Breakfast

Humans salivate for property

swinish lust for pearls, gaza stripping

all the King's mines, hyena territory.

This much the world's made useless.

And still we scythe the greensward

close and now are sheepishly

for slaughter, ready for the drains.

Boys and girls, there's no longer covenant,

no hopeful promise of any ark this time.

Nor Noah, no, not this time but some sudden

fright instead coming around the corner.

The revenue man coming for back taxes.

J.B. Cooper on his banana bike, scattering

all, all--sick to death of his balloons.

Couple

The Gulf Coast

Lumbering tourists swell to flight
with pelicans above the Odyssey Motel.
Siren wagons gather passengers from
the ships whitening Tampa Bay.

Here cruise directors offer syntax
for salvation, here are fountains
for our wrinkled childhoods, and here
we shower in gold dust before we sleep.

And bask in cobalt blue among the mangroves.
But this I only dream, lying wet with fear,
to hear the muffled prehistoric roar of TV
beasts, Godzilla and the priests . . .

Remember how we fought waist-deep
at Lauderdale, how we swung at Sebring,
where bones and dried leather hang gibbeted.
Nobody's at home at Nixon's place.

The airconditioning turns off automatically.
I tear away my skin to eat an orange and see
above the sky footprints huge as bigtop clowns
run by tinsel-hatted mice. I awake without

egrets. So what if my white innocence's flown,
and what I didn't know has left me nothing
else to think or do -- except to cruise the Ever-
glades, flashlight ready for the perfect

crystal fake, sold by Seminoles. No matter
that my compass rose has wilted. I will find
the lost keys to my budget car sunk in the muck
of hamburgers and chicken fried along

the reeking causeways, arching the golden flood.
Where frightened tourists, clutching their Konicas
and bonded rum against the end, run in panic
as the Great Wallenda loses balance in the fog

and falls. And my Eldorado's almost out of gas.
But the airport says they can see to fly.
So just in time by early light I catch at twice
the cost the last plane to the Coast.

My sample case is safely stuffed with baby gators.

Warrior

Householding

I am my own yellowpages.
I am the plumber, call me
son-of-stillson, but I know
secretly, no easy way fixes
anything--soaped drawers always
stick, fixed faucets still drip,
leak back or up, through the floor.
It's all one in the woods.
It's urban/rural here, haven slum
for squirrels and mice, who even
now confetti up the walls, while
the ants picnic in the roofbeams.
Some day we'll houseproof it all.
That bird we saw the other day --
not the vulture but the warbler --
gives us hope.

Portrait of the Artist

In 50 Words Or Less: After X Why Z?

Whose stitch in time saves mine, Hawkins wandered?

Rough ribbed on prairie seas he scratched himself

for fleas, he Hawkins, feelingly--the rigors of mortis

setting in, those coffee blues, that doomsday feeling.

Hawkins remembered the strangest apples bitten

to the root of matter on the backside of the moon.

And now he might as well (as Fate) slouch on

to Beaverton for late connections, for tea and toast.

Birds nesting in the soup--now for the pouring:

Nothing of egregious errors. Peccadillos only.

No more flying saucers or at the most no Hex.

All this for him has been a silk purse of years at best.

But now unleashed and on the scent he plays for Zed.

Portrait of the Artist as a Young Man, Too

It Turns Out Even Old Dogs Earn New Spots

Not much has changed since you were gone:

The cats less sullen, gardens more refulgent--

the old velocities of spring. We are still

economizing by turning back the dogs,

who even now earn new spots.

There are still some puzzles between

the heaves of storm, certain intermittencies.

Like the owlish opacity of goats swiveling

their necks and eating everything in sight,

sweeping low, regurgitating all the rest.

Our accountant will verify this publicly.

Margot, you'll be glad to know, runs

for a whole year on half a lemon. Primavera!

P.S. I'll meet you at the station. Say Zen.

Viking Warrior Helmed

NA.MATH

mach.ining 3.000
perfect passes
reached the moon
touched 1st 2nd 3rd
came home before any.
body else then col.
lapsed 7 mins. short
of a mi. breathing

VI.VAL.DI

Dead Viking Warrior

Mt. Time

Dear Wife,

Classes are out. There's time.
Half our kids are coasting Mexico,
the other half hauled out in Boston.
You're in Tucson, meeting. So.
Now is better time than any to paint
you Hood, how trillium unfurls and ice
lets go the whiskey sound of jays
sanding the noisy woods. You remember.
Body to the sun, the chill goes off
the skin. Turning back, it's mountain
cold again. We both remember.

A worm of climbers inches up,
roped the final feet against the white
and disappears, circled by an albatross
I think, but see it is a plane,
even smaller from below.

That high we'd want to ski the clouds,
jump the Rockies and sail the jetstream.
At thirty thousand feet the listening
tubes are blue, the wine is very good,
the Mozart even better. You know that.

But now I see the wind has changed.

Tomorrow, if you're back, in the maple
falling air and easy drift of stars,
like chameleons, we'll change our fires
for other sails and bend the wind
another way.

I'll get celestial bends from this imagining.

Your husband.

Viking Warrior Saved

Peace Time Army

Coming down a long corridor,
the tall general in a jacket named after him.
The war is over. We are doing the paperwork.

Eating Hersheys and drinking Coke.

Telling the veterans how to adjust
To civilian life. Filling out forms.

We are eighteen. They are tolerant.

The Supreme Commander pauses,
asks what state, son, but mostly
he talks with the veterans, quietly.
Blue eyes. Big grin. Later he is President.

Like Grant and the other wartime generals.

The war has unwound.

Our NCO's only pretend to be tough.

Everyone is getting out.

That was all a long time ago.

Today I can only dimly remember Hitler,
his moustache infinitesimal in time.

But Ike's blue eyes still insist.

The Military-Industrial Complex

is still his warning.

Dancers

Long Distance Winter

I heard this morning how my mother caught
six mice under the sink in one cold week.
Then two birds came down the chimney, black with soot.
As to the mice, that's good huswifery and bodes well.
But about the birds the omens are not so clear.
I had a vision how, with Dad no longer there,
she'd snared them in a web of loneliness, fashioned
from her widowhood, and turned the starvelings out.

Later today my wife encountered a great brown bear
in the park next to the library, where she's doing
research on aging. Also a resourceful woman like Mother,
she simply climbed a tree and waited until the bear
lost interest and turned into a small trout, silver
as the grass. At this season, stranger things have happened.

Torso

Reparation

Knee we knelt to knee
and felt the chill
of summer risk--
our sixteen years together
stretched six thousand miles
to France and back.
Still worlds apart
and hanging by our words,
we tangled yeas and nays.
She was giving most
though I was saying most
in strung-out words
of blame for loneliness--
until we closed the space
that follows separation.

Amadeus

Lot's Wife Had Plenty To Be Angry About

Like, his family (lots of Lots) were always looking back
so concerned about heritage and family name -- and if any
one happened to be in the line of sight -- look out for them,
the relatives -- they had turned a lot of people into salt.
Dwelling too much on their own importance, thinking power.

Like, one cousin (Lot's, not his wife's) not a look alike but he
looked a lot like Lot, went grasping for the right metaphor
(at a family dinner) to praise them up and said:
"You are all the salt of the earth," that's how he began.

Then he made a big mistake,"You are all pillars of society,"
he said, and then everyone began to salinate, salinate, salinate.
It was hereditary. She (Lot's wife) knew it. They all knew it.
But that did not stop happening what happened: It was their lot.

47

American Family

Scanning The Horizon For Whales

Today we celebrate
The Patron Saint of Wales,
she called out from the bathroom.

I imagine cetaceans.
The Saint feeding the whales?

No, she called over the water. Wales.

Calling back and forth, enjoying how
she's used to my pretending not to hear:
Whales or Wales--no cross purposes-
we're enjoying being downtown
at a friend's apartment, unpacking.

I bought three pairs of panties
and two pairs of gloves, she tells me.

Why would you do that? Why have brought?

No, she says, I bought three pairs. On Sale.

And then she told me the doctor
had examined her, and she was fine.

How did he look, I asked?

Dark hair, she said, topsiders
and grey socks like yours, that slump down.

No, I mean how did he examine you?

And we both could laugh at that, too,
because we had been worried.

I liked the whale part best.

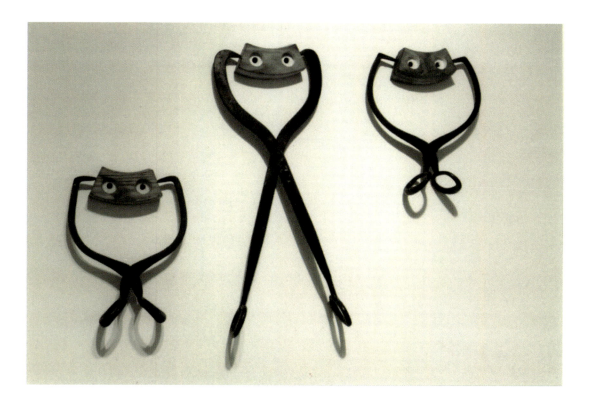

The Tong Dynasty

Other People's Children (1969)

The other day a moist infestation
of other people's children hanging
in their cloggy nests reminded me
of our own grub-fed fledglings,
of their indifferent greed and how
I would often don iridescent robes
of purple age and wish them flown.

Other People's Children (1987)

The other day I spied
a moist infestation
of other people's children
hanging from their cloggy nests.
This reminded me of our own
grub-fed fledglings and their
indifferent greed and how I
would often don iridescent robes
of purple age and wish them flown.
Now I wish them home -- these others grown.

Jack's Spats

Slouching

towards
Beaverton
half
dragged
from one
world
to the next
we glimpse
Leda on her
swan
at the local
drive-in
the audience
gasping horror:
fearful
mutancy
all beak
no wings --
dodo issue
from their
union.
No longer song
just squeak.

Dancers

This World Is Much Too Much Perhaps

Here's Goldilocks again complaining

about the porridge and smashing furniture.

After such a meager diet of horizon

who can blame her? She's a city girl, you know.

Has never seen a cow hand milked. (Who has?)

What does she care about Botticelli?

Or how the three bears must feel coming

home to find their place wrecked up?

It could have been so good with her breasts

like painted hills chiseled in the sky.

The hummingbird would perceive her nectar even.

She could be Flora and we who are smoldering

on the edge of distinction would be her newest lover.

But first we'd check to see our gizzards were intact.

Conversant Birds

Tick Ripe For Bursting

There are a lot of things under my saddle

I don't like, but saying what they are is

like trying to focus a camera after you've

dropped it. Besides, I shouldn't complain.

I'm the one who's always taking off his clothes

for the CIA, trying to tell everything at once

and then falling through my own language.

Better to keep your eyes on the rim of truth

over the edge of the plate, much better

than being like a tick ripe for bursting

and then keening when it happens.

Stand back. I feel another confession coming on.

Stripped bare, the oo's and ah's may save us.

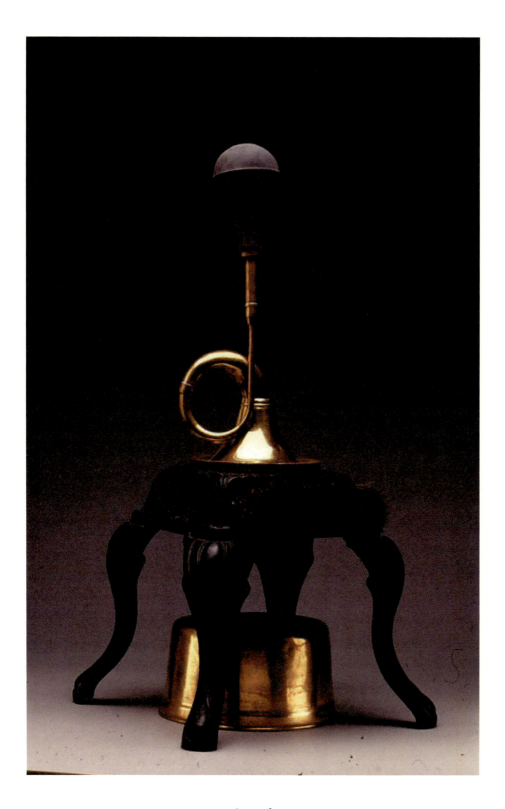

Sounder

Trying To Get Scarpia Out Of A Deep Hole

Candles in each hand, not at his head this time.
He loved beauty and hearing arias, both to his credit.
The yellow pages of his fevered imagination are now
crinkled with time, but I will be his alter ego, with him
at the altar of his discontent — he wanted more than
seeing beauty, needed the having of it, and he could
have been an A+ in musical appreciation, the way
he was in the middle of the scene, well costumed.

But he used the wrong tactics, almost as though he
did have a tin ear, immune to the nuances, the trills
the sharps and flats needed for proper plotting.
He just botched up the scenario with his sleazy
behind the scenes finding ways to "off" the hero
and have the heroine all to his very sexy own.

This is a sort of write in vote for him, Scarpia:
Bad guy, through and through, but you know
the adage about the way good can come of evil.
I mean the way Verdi did it (no, you idiot — I mean
Puccini) the way he made the opera and TOSCA.
If only Scarpia had listened to his own inner ear
he might have developed perfect pitch and turned
everything upside down and won her for his own.

Reconfiguration

Unidentified Sources

Spokesman said, who spoke
on condition, said one intelligence
source said . . .
Chairman, who did not elaborate,
said plane
just flew into mountain.
Others, who declined to be identified,
also said heavy rains . . .
fully authorized . . . under contract
a specific period of time . . .
applicable procedures . . .
next of kin . . .

We are the Hollow Men

Who Carved These Runes

Captain Hook and me we wander in the bloomin'

trades looking for our leader, druid of the desert.

We've gathered round the rock telling rooster tales,

decomposing sermons to ourselves and feeling lonesome

scaley underfoot, for the dragon he's beguiled us

since we ate of that imperfect deed of fruit.

"Ne me touche pas," we think but it does and we are

falling through the cracks where we have built our

selves a tower for to see (blind mutants that we are)

the sea, the shadow line at least beyond the surf.

Oddsbodkinman, he surely should appear to us

for we must know who carved these runes.

At least we thought he ought, for we remember

his gardens as imperfect gifts that rarely ripen.

Ma and Pa Chairs

Wilderness

We are in a hidden place.
All nitre, moss and seepage.
Trying to remember what
we should have kept
when all else was gone.
Magpie hungers.
I have been thinking, she says
about how our hungers bind us.
We have only a little left
of all the Halloween candy
we've been carrying.
It's easy to eat too many
all at once.

The craving for salt
is much stronger now
after so many days.
The thought of cigarettes
twists our tongues.
There are more pressing hungers.
But the walls are closing
in on us, about to implode
like an old TV on an ash heap.
We are now in the seventh day.
I can think of no alternatives.
Any more talk would bury us.
Outside the tundra heaves
and flashes like broken glass.
The air blinds our eyes.

Flotsam